THE GOSPEL OF UNMADE CREATION

THE GOSPEL OF UNMADE CREATION

THABANI TSHUMA

RECENT
WORK
PRESS

The Gospel of Unmade Creation
Recent Work Press
Canberra, Australia

Copyright © Thabani Tshuma, 2023

ISBN: 9780645651294 (paperback)

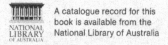

A catalogue record for this
book is available from the
National Library of Australia

Cover image: from 'Gulf of Mexico' by the US Geographical Service via unsplash
Cover design: Recent Work Press
Set by Recent Work Press

recentworkpress.com

ss

For Max Tshuma,
who taught me how to create my own world

Contents

Gravitas

There is gravitas in
beginnings

and opening lines.
          Points of entry.

The wondering where to start, when
we are already there.

It is over once
          we name it.

So
we suspend ourselves

          in-between

the body.

In flesh, sweat, sinew and linen.

In the weaving of postponement.

We are made of mixed procrastinating limbs.

Deluded into forgetting
all this time we have is not enough.

Time,
        like skin,
when stretched,   wrinkles.

All the imperfections
become harbingers of wisdom.
And starting becomes
a
    protracted
                way
                    to
                end.

How to be Thabani (a list poem)

1. Don't. I've tried it and it's a horrendous idea.

2. If you must, start with an accent, not the one you were born with, a mutated version you adopted in order to assimilate and be understood.

3. Grow up in Zimbabwe, ignore the fact that it's difficult to do. Also, ignore that it isn't the obvious starting point of this list because when you're him, cultural identity becomes quite misplaced and malleable.

4. Learn a bunch of other social concepts and constructs— masculinity, capitalism, democracy, mismanaging mental health, something along the lines of distorted self-image, and believe them to be true even if they do a disservice to you.

5. Fuel your life with coconut oil, use it in your hair, on your skin, to cleanse your wounds, as a substitute for lube- -ricating the pan you use to cook your food! (I usually use olive oil).

6. Drink heavily and do ALL the drugs

7. Do number 6 again for good measure.

8. Do number 6 again out of habit.

9. Do number 6 again just to feel something.

10. Go to rehab. You'll hate it at first, that won't go away the whole time you're there. But what happens next will save your life.

11. Unlearn those social concepts and constructs you adopted in number 4

12. Write poetry. Most of it will be self-indulgent bullshit, like list poems about how to be you, but some of it might actually be dope, and someone might relate. So keep writing.

13. Forgive your parents—they're only human and some humans really do do the best they can. They did.

14. Forgive yourself—you're only human and some humans really do do the best they can. You did.

15. Have impeccable taste in fashion, dress for the mirror, which is to say wear what makes you happy and extend it as a metaphor beyond clothing that encompasses your whole life.

16. Remember number 1, and how being me is horrendous idea? Be you instead, it's a beautiful thing and probably a better list poem.

Drought Season

The sky sheds no tears for my country.
Kicked-up dust no longer settles—
it lingers
in air clouded by perceptions of difference.
An insistent incense ritualistically burned
gives off fumes that intoxicate with disdain and unrest.
A so-called chosen people that worship unblessed.
An innocence lost as mother nature was undressed.
Her now barren womb stands to attest,
that the fruits of one's labour are the chains of the oppressed.
I nomadically stand as a man dispossessed.
My humble behest to confess,
the sky sheds no tears for my country.

Chapped, cracking lips beg to be kissed
by the reminiscent cool a fresh rain mist,
from time undefined by the words coexist
when being was nature and living was This.
Before outstretched hands were curled into fists,
and the boundaries of land were all but dismissed.
Those once picturesque vistas, now painted in blood.
I would cry.
But even the sky sheds no tears for my country.

She booms!
A thunderclap applause to pause despair.
Where,
the swelling bags under her blue eyes are silver-lined.
Her sunsets dance with palettes of warmth

mingling in the hills from southeast to the north.
in beauty that defies proclamation of worth.
She says:
Love me or not, I will be as I am.
And be here long after the saga of man.
Burdened but not saddened in your plight to be free.
For I, as The Sky,
shed no tears for your country.

Dancing Awkwardly in the Rain

I have forgotten the feel of rain on my skin.
Although,
I shower daily. Perhaps to purge the stench
of this decay:
the reason I am clean.
Something about the rain seems like assault.
A molestation of unwanted wetness.
Nature's wanton tears.

We enter, seeking the source of growth
and exit damp,
disgruntled and unrewarded.
How beautiful it is to drown in such
careless falling.
Exalting our septic lungs.

I prefer the memories of drought,
abrasive in their dryness,
chaffing thirsty flesh.

When water was so scarce,
we took cold showers.

How to Fail: A saga

I dreamt I forgot my speech
while being awarded
a participation trophy.
In waking life,
I'm equally clumsy,
expressing gratitude for having fun.

I do not enjoy involvement
but enjoy being   uninvolved.
It remains unsolved and
the problem is
unpoetic.

I use excessive negation
for the nonchalant aesthetic.
          Prettier for caring less.
Simultaneously careless.

Awkward saying goodbye
because I never want to leave.
Unsure how best to say:

Please Stay.

Not forever.
Maybe,
a couple of minutes more?

Cups are known for running over and
my social skills are poor.

There's that smile again

All, curling lip corners and teeth.
Such hopeful, tender joy,
concealing mischief underneath.
As unintentionally charming
as the things I often dream.
And then forget
the point was only to have fun.

Origami Origins

Watch,
as this unfolds itself.
An animated origami object
undoing its creation.

Wanting nothing more
than to be paper.
It was always paper
until we made it something else.

Blank before the fold.
Blank before the ink dance
or cursor blink.
Let there be

nothing.

Followed by six days of rest.
And a seventh, reserved for penance
proportional to plagiarised piety.

The gospel of un-made things.

We do not pray for born saints here.
Revere the slate,
as unblemished as blackness.
Castigate the Actors playing
God.

Redact the word G*d from colloquial use,
store it in a sacristy for future use
in blasphemy
and other tricks of truth.

As for me? (Or you)

The same as always will be:
a predestined damnation.

(Darn! *Dante was onto something*)

'Nine circles' always had a nice ring:
a matrimonial conclusion.

We, the dead, do our part
in unbecoming.

Jungle Book

I once wished I was raised by wolves.
Not to forsake my mother or father,
but rather,
to have an origin story that would warrant being a little wild.
As a child, I was,
a tad awkward:
a gangly stalk that walked with two left feet.

Like an unsprung spring, wound tense and taut, too tight to trip, but
    still falling.
My balance offset by a constant sense of insecurity.
A quintessential need to not be me.

My father—
he always taught me to be more sheep than wolf.
Although HIS method was more about appearing sheathed in wool:
play the stoic role, mask with emotional disguise.
Wear it! to the point that you cease to recognise
whether **This Guy** is the real you or the social role you adopted.
I stopped it.
To avoid the inevitable existential quandaries,
that for centuries have been the squandering of far greater
    philosophical minds than mine,
For to deny my nature would be to deny the very thing that makes
    me human.
But remember,
this man-cub once wished he was raised by Wolves.

Because Younger Me was a loner,
with a lingering longing to join a pack, or pride or herd.
To be one of the vainglorious birds of a feather,
with the simple pleasure of flocking off together.
The choice to weather every storm with each other—
with sisters and brothers.

My Mother—
Her methodology was a macabre blend of the meticulous and
   ridiculous.
Distorted into myth by time.
I, in the dual role of Romulus and Remus
seeking Augury. On beaten wings,
murdering my shadow self and twin,
to learn that Rome wasn't built in a day,
but one day at a time.
And a licking is only defeat,
when wounds are left unattended.

My parents were splendid.
And despite them or maybe to spite them,
I grew up to be a lone wolf.
A pack just wasn't conducive to defining or re-defining my truth.

I'm finding the hunt, though, is harder.
Each meal is a battle, for just desserts
where the proof is in the putting down of anything I'm attached
to.

I've had to see that wild and tame,
live in the same symbiotic polarity as night and day.
Too late to trade a soul for the safe illusion
of being raised by wolves.

Thoughts on 'Home'

Born on no man's land, I became a nomadic traveller.
My shoes, dusted with the red dirt of Mashonaland.
They say the crimson pigment is a post-war blood staining.
What use are roots when the soil is infertile?
I am dry land driftwood,
contours cracked with time.
Toxic to burn.
Twice shy
to the flames.

Call this home.
Call me home.
Take me home.

Hold on.
Wait
a little
longer.
We exist to serve the interest of our people.
More for you is less for us
You chose to come, and stay by the grace we grant.
The grace we took, the grace they built, the grace we spilt.

Is this home?
Am I home?
Take me home.

I choke.
Sputter to
speak. Spat out
by the fumes that consume this place.
Barbed wire borders lacerating to the bone.
What use is a passport when its pages are sanctioned?
I am an unwelcome passenger still fighting to stay.
A hopeful ghost haunting the same empty place as predecessors.

                              Where is home?
                              Are you home?
                              Take me home.

                                        Come.
                                  Realise your
                                       dreams.
                                         Here.
                    Wholesale warehouses are filled with freedom.
                  Take your pick of a path to greater opportunity.
                            Leave behind the anguish of your origins.
                This is our land, we welcome you to call it home.

I miss home.
There is no home.
Take me home.

I long for a place that no longer exists.
Yearn for shoes caked in red dirt.
A reminder of the journey past.
Take steps towards tomorrow's earthy promise.

What use is land if uninhabited?
The still sun sets on the savannah.
I still smell the rain.
It smells like

Home.
Home.
Home.

16

We Never Called it 'Prom'

Our high-school dance.
We're young and nervous,
bold and reckless.
Think this is the most alive we'll ever be.
I'm glad you picked me.

I have ink for saliva and felt-tip teeth,
prone to write instead of speaking,
And yet, you hear me.
You,
The girl who is a little too radiant to pass for human,
hiding flaws that mute your halo.
I carve hieroglyphs of this dance with you into my memory walls—
preserve as this perfect moment.

We fast forward a short time,
to me, bespectacled with bursting capillaries and tears.
That boy that I was—abandoned,
strung out, and stranded.
Less than half the man I could be,
consumed by all that I would not be.
Barely able to clearly see you.
And yet, you see me.

Your once muted halo shines a light.
I follow.
Close burning eyes and remember that dance.
It's a reason, one of many, to keep going.
The hope that among the madness,
another dance with you could happen.

Between Two Points

Here
is in the exact same place as
after someone whose name sounded
thunderous applause in praise of
you left a wound that scarred like
sandpaper smoothed the grain, we
cut, and back to one.
After
life is but a
dream a little lie because of
me, myself and death
become undone. It was the night of our lives and
I'm having something I can't pronounce. It sounds
like attracts the things we hate about
ourselves.
It's fireflies in the summer
time and time again mistakes were
made in the only place that still sells
hope can break a heart like nothing
else or other options, take your
pick my bones before they turn to
ash.

G-Note

It is 2006.
My only ambition is to own a PS3.
I am terrified of growing up.
Pluto is apparently not a planet anymore.
Small things have a way of being forgotten,
or reclassified.

My sister says 'You gotta listen to this'.
She is older so her taste is better (allegedly).
From a place of grace, or power, or the need to educate,
she lends me her boombox (we called them 'radios')
and MCR's *The Black Parade* album.

Cue that G-note.

Cue spine tingle, halted breath,
mouth as a gaping vacuum,
rapid-fire blinking,

I just might cry.

I am not yet a punk rock fan.
Think, 'I have just become a punk rock fan.'
Think, 'Life was incomplete before this band'.
I do not say Stan yet, but in hindsight—Stan that!
And understand the power of an instrumental procession.
The howl of raging vocals,
the divine ecstasy of anthems.

It is 2008.
Death decides it is time we get acquainted.
Arrives uninvited.
Lingers under a new name, grief.
I play 'Welcome to the Black Parade' on repeat.
I cry.
I cry.
I cry.
I stop crying.
The song keeps playing.

It is 2012.
I'm searching for a subculture,
learning how to ricochet between identities—
unnoticed due to constant motion.
In the pause:
I question belonging.
My hair, too nappy for a fringe.
My father's refrain:
'No son of mine will ever wear eyeliner.'
But,
My skin keeps me dressed in all **black.**
And what could be more Emo than that?

It is 2018.
What a band they were!
The disbanded architects of our memories.
We talk about how some songs are timeless.
I gratuitously use the word 'eclectic' to describe my taste.
What I mean to say is:
I am afraid,

and chaotic, soulful, rhythmic, psychedelic, enchanted, enchanting,
   guffawing,
a teenage-adult, at odds with living
and so very much alive.

It is 2020.
She tells me, 'It is a funeral song.'
Agrees it is the sound of intravenous emotion.
The tones linger in our marrow.
We have always been dying.

What a glorious thing it is
to carry on

In Line

Draw me a line.
Not in a substance or on a surface,
not to set a limit—
just a line.

See how everything we have is constructed from lines.
Guided by maps made of lines.
Travelling on roads that are long lines.
Feigned connection by phone lines.
Sometimes fading our own lines.
We're outlines. And without lines?
Would we reach for a lifeline?

Even this line,
means nothing without the lines set before it.
An obscure line in loneliness,
unfinished before its deadline.

I'm inclined to find that tender line.
That quick to sketch but slow to render line.
Giving space to write an ending line,
~~In time.~~

Bio-poem

Their name is too soft to touch most tongues.
AKA a whisper.
Also known as words you wished were said out loud.
AKA phonetic kisses.
They come from Home, although spend most of their time trying
   to get back there, forgetting they never left.
They used to be louder but now live by library rules.
They know they are a vibration
that can be felt in the bones at the right frequency.
They want to be a voice
as opposed to just a sound.
They wish they could be the music that quiets the noise.
They need amplification.
They have a half-decent speaker system.
They love that so much of life moves in waves.
They hate that light travels faster.
They are happy that silence holds so much power.
Their name is something you'll hear if you listen.
And that is all that matters.

This is not a heartbreak

We talk of the piece torn out:
the fleshy pulp.
Of the hole it left.
The cavern.
Of hand, knife, claw
or other ripping things.

We talk some more.
Blood dries the way paint does—
boring to watch.
We scar, or heal, or die,
or talk some more.

And let he who is without reflection
skim the first stone across the surface.
And then forget,
as we do,
just how little time we have always had.
And how long a waiting
can hurt.

Runaways

We are the kids who ran away from home,
slung rucksacks full of dreams
over heavy-laden shoulders.
Stepped into the night,
skies speckled with potential fears.
We, the mildly unafraid,
see them as guiding lights,
luminous with possibilities.

We walk.
Appear to the observer's eye to have little direction.
We wondrous wanderers embracing wanderlust.
Aren't lost.
A stone's throw away   is farther when you skip it.
So we skimmed miles across oceans.
Grew from hoping to knowing,
each brush on the water's surface could be used
to paint the cerulean hues of infrequent moons.
Dancing to both tunes of artist and muse.
In finding, we inspired ourselves.

Grounded, chasing mountains to match.
Inured to rocky paths, scorched while blazing trails,
turned blisters into callouses,
and photographs into forever.
With a bindle bundled at the end of a stick,
we're quick to be mistaken for homeless,
forgetting we made the choice to leave.
We didn't just run away from home,
we're running towards it.

The Prodigal Son

My father was a gambling man.
Like the old song goes, like his father before.
Like me, as the rising sun, built on sand instead of stone.
Perhaps this is not a proper poem.
Or
does it only cease to be after announcing that?
Was there a moment before it?
In the silence
the stuttering misstep untaken, for the sake of not breaking a promise.
I was promised the world once.

So, I sowed my dreams as seeds,
and buried them in the depths of me for all eternity.
And
perhaps you've heard of me?

I am known to some as the prodigal son.
I left with no intent to return, but intentions left unattended
tend to burn the hopes they hold in their wake.
Make no mistake,
I played my hand to chance with a flick of heads or tails to wish me
    well.
I now dare to dwell too long on the past,
fervently intoxicated by nostalgia.
Memories,
unlike those buried dreams,
have a longer life expectancy.
They plague us with their haunting joys,
and fears we don't expect to see.

Shut eyes would see as spectres see,
if sleep could bring me peace.

I'm puzzled—
in pieces.
The fractals reflect varying spectrums to place me upon.
They beg may the prodigal son be raised,
akin to light,
Though weighed by skin as dark as night,
To be brighter than the snowy glow it wished to imitate.
Yet missed the spinning loom of fate, a grasp to reach too little too
    late.
To be swallowed for the things you hate,
but hate to love,

I gave everything I had,
to be enough
And then gave a little more to feel in love.
The same visceral yet satirical slice
of comedy and tragedy that spurred,
Alighieri's quest through hell to paradise,
by way of seven-layered sins.
Incited since by nature's abhorrence of vacuums,
where every empty throne must have a king.
Magnificent, resplendent
but ultimately as false the gods would ordain.
And would such pain have paupers call for regal praise?
For a subtle touch of royal cloth to cure the world's malaise,
As if it could.

As if my darlings were not so long deceased that killing them
    would be redundancy.

And my heroes turned out to be mortal, flawed and fallible.

The invaluable lessons are learnt, and I'm wary to make a return.
To the moment it started, as two lips parted,
And uttered
'Son, go live out your poem'.

A River God's Wrath

Let history remember the toll of turning water into lightning.

I will whisper this
slowly fading oral tradition to my children.
From a time before Time. When
Zambezi's raging rapids belonged to Nyami Nyami,

elemental protector of the BaTonga people.
His daunting primeval form, seldom seen by mortals.
The gargantuan head of a fish
a body defying measurement.
Serpentine, so say sagacious elders
whose glossed eyes once glimpsed him.

His presence
would reverse the river current,
His infinite meandering laid out a regal red carpet
darkening the water's vermillion flow.
The valley's virescent growth was owed to his grace.
Water means life to nature.
Oblation to him reaped fertility's reward.
Benevolent, He would offer his own flesh to sate the starving.
A spirit of equal parts compassion and wrath,
concurrently consumed with adoration of his wife,
unnamed as a lesser deity,
blessing Kariwa Gorge.

An overshadowed love story

In remembrance

I will condole the
backbreaking burden of progress.
From a time that changed Time.
When the men without knees sought to harness the river's power.
Men with ivory skin and the sky's blue trapped in their eyes.
Men of equal ambition
and hubris.
Who with steel and mortar, subdued nature's grandeur.
Zambezi's torrential waters walled in by Kariba Dam.
An affront to Nyami Nyami.

Families and fauna displaced
in the sojourning name of development.
Each construction attempt torn down by colossal floods,
the fury of a River God.

Undeterred, the dogged ashen men rebuilt it,
again,
and again,
and again,
persistant to conquer.
Rising water, when forced, means death to nature.

The dam that defied a god.

Forged on a foundation of bodies swept into cement.
A splitting schism creating a forlorn deity,
his wife forever trapped on the other side.

An ancient spirit retreats.
His people tell his story to their children.
They carve his likeness in Mopani wood.
Caution against currents of crashing white
foam.

I will honour the solemn duty
to remember forgotten Gods.
In a time to come,
when the spirits, Vadzimu,
rattle the borders between worlds.
The River God's wrath will rise.
With broken bricks beholden to the past,
man-made walls will fall.

And his people find home
on the riverbank once more.

N'anga

Who made the meaning?
Who gave the meaning?
Who changed the meaning?

The search for more, was meaning – less.
They told them, ~~God~~
was dead.
They called him ~~Devil,~~
instead.
They called her ~~Witch.~~

Doctored history as we remember it.
The books bare little semblance to the truth.
You!
I remember you.

Silver tongue, dripping in sacred sooth.
Cave drawn, in stone-walled scrawling.
Whistled as a vision of the future present.
A monotheistic past.

Greetings,
To   Vadzimu, The Ancestors.
You were US before We became We.
Before the social schism to Them
Before ME.
I died,
And met a trickster deity, he wore my face in jest,
Had spider limbs for legs

And my lifespan wound as Web.
All so sickly sticky as silk spun thread.
As a memory,
in remembrance of forgetting.
As a child, bastardised at birth.
A Sun eclipsed by The Moon of New ~~God~~,
A So-called One True ~~God~~
I am not made in His image.

What was theirs and what was ours?
What was light and what was stars?

Who made the meaning?
Who gave the meaning?
Who changed the meaning?

History favours the Hunter not the hunted.
I will be unapologetic
in incantation.
A tongue before speech could seek throat.
A guttural roar on golden plains.
The loose lip that slipped the chains.
To reclaim the oral capacity,
to see through the blinding opacity.
To cast a new truth.

To make the meaning.
To take the meaning.
To give the meaning.
To change the meaning.
To be all that we were meant to be.
And more.

Emergence

A reinterpreted idiom.
An abstract hand holds the pan.
I panhandle for mercy.
The heat is turned up.
Cue mild concern and correct attribution
of calefaction to the stove.

The pan only conducts, but I'm frying anyway.

Black absorbing heat has more to do with
wavelength than temperature.
Regardless, hot is hot.
And I've not forgotten how I got here.
The hand holding the pan plays the role of enforcer.
Unwarranted but suffered from.
With hiss and spit, I think
how fitting this sizzling end.

I have always been framed for consumption.

Close my eyes in resignation.
Then,
in a last-minute twist of fate,
with all the cruelty of hope,
am tossed into the fire.

From one from of incineration to another.
Some claim, the fire is worse.
I make this burning a re-birth,
refuse to be fuel and instead transmute.
Consume that abstract hand that threw me in.
Take its body, like it took mine.
Role reversed retribution
in the reduction to blackness and ashes.

A wave of awakened ancient anger
spanning generations of scorched souls.
A choking smoulder turned inferno
in divine comedic justice, void of malice.

This new form is fury in its purest
roaring in all its incendiary glory.
You will not soon forget my name.

Once thrown out of the frying pan,
I become the flame.

Broomstrokes

It is swept under the rug.
Brushed dust that one could only see
once it is gathered.
That would otherwise linger in
unspoken air.

Discarded

micro-particles of a greater whole.
Begging beyond the surface to dive
into a deep clean sweep of absolution.
The dirt they washed their hands of,
yet forgot how it clings to the skin.
A thin veneer, both protective and pollutant.
Its echoing stain, the sound of offhand remarks.

Removed,

to return again in time.
If these broom strokes were brush strokes,
the rug, a white canvas,
the layered paint would leave no room
For dust to settle.

s(K)IN

Will this be history?
The loudness, the silence,
the white
noise.
Today does not arrive the way we dreamt.

I peel these words from the blank
space   between hesitation.
With a childlike clumsiness.
In a transmuted tongue
swallowed hoping to be understood.
Salivating slick with silver,
the smelted thirty pieces of betrayal.
Sifted through stolen soil.
Handled with sandpaper palms.
Some hands
stay bloody.

My hands
have the velvet delicacy of partial privilege.
Double-edged
as tenderness and shame.
Exhausting to a fault.
I have not always been tired.
but,
I have always been black.

Have heard the sound of this anguish
in quiet desperation.

In palletised platitudes.
In hertz,
as the cycles of waves in time.

'Now' was,
and in ceaseless spills,
is the time.
A rewriting of that history.
This time,
not by the so-called victors,
but by the grave-born.
In the name of every murdered premature ancestor.

This be midnight!
The rumbling timbre, the pinpoint pitch.
The Bass
drop.
Bones have been weary far too long.
I feel it in my (s)kin.

Message in a Bottle

The stock price of *Talk* changed.

It's still cheap.

But it got louder.
The buzz makes it hard to hear,
so I wrote you a message in a bottle.

The practice was

familiar,
similar to the stacked Tupperware,
awkwardly holding my emotions.
I'm an expert at fitting things
in vessels they don't belong.

It's not wrong,

just the best way to get by.
(I tell myself to get by.)
You never said goodbye,
and I resent you for it.

That pain too is boxed away.
I store it right behind the trillion things
I never got to say.
Like,
how you smell of vanilla and coconut.
And how now,
I hate them both.
I have discovered that the people who survive,
become the ghosts.
We trade our peace
for you to rest in.
Damned to watch our hurting lessen.

To never truly know,
what's moving on or what's forgetting.

Back to the message:

The first line said
'I'm sorry. Don't worry.
I'll be fine'.
I followed that with an immediate admittance
I was lying.
What came next might be blurred out,

I find it hard to write while crying.

Perhaps the tears and ink
simply says 'I love you'.
I chose brevity,
the way you always nagged me to.
Sealed the bottle like a secret,
with a whisper, not a kiss.
I didn't toss it in the ocean,
I'm far too worn for futile hope.
Instead, I stored it in the place,
I put my dreams, my fears and oaths.

In the most special part of me.

Little Spoon

So there's this guy.
For the sake of continuity let's call him '*Me*'.
Chest puffed out, broad wingspan shoulders,
a towering 6'2 and I LOVE
to be the little spoon.
That's not entirely true,
I'm actually closer to 5'11.
Apply resume rules to height
(I excel a little more on paper.)
They say the truth is far stranger than fiction.
I am articulate in exaggerating diction.
Which means,
the mode I use says what I mean.
Is more than the median mediocre.
And immediately,
like high school geometry homework,
I am prone to a tangent.
But
back to the narrative at hand,
to, '*the guy*' or '*me*',
or an aptly placed placeholder in the metaphorical form,
that LOVES to be the little spoon.

To set the scene:

A fluid body, spills into mattress bowl
longing for that curving cradle comfort.
Labelled as ladel-like.
Often mistakenly portrayed as lady-like.

And the guy, known as *me*.
is known to bite off more than he can chew,
is framed to be consumed.
It's ironic that he would be seen as any kind of spoon,
that's   food for thought.

I bend myself in bed.
I find the night can be intoxicating.
I soiree with dusk.
Take up day drinking for sobriety.
Sleepwalking for cardio.
Gain an appreciation
for exercises in futility.
Long overdue in doing my due diligence.
As the proverb goes:
The prodigal son burns down the village to feel the warmth.
Oh, how those nights were cold.
And Dark.
And Dreamless.
The succeeding transition was seamless,
from pillow talk to meaning,
to '*the guy*', to '*me*', to '*a scene*',
to a spoon too small to hold a hearty helping of soul,
too big to sleep in the bed it made,
too meta to make any sort of self-referential sense.

Soliloquy meets commentary,
they fall in love.
In the same way similarly dissimilar things do—

Paradoxically.

Like poetry as—
prose with more line breaks.

and a line that takes a little more to write
than it does to say out loud.
Like how
I LOVE to be the little spoon!!!
Tend towards tenderness
to koala wrap its limbs around me.
Just to sleep soundly.
Not with another body,

I'm in bed with all the different ways I present,
just wishing one
would hold me.

Ghostwriter

Ummm Hi?
I'm Thabani's ghost writer.

That sounds weird.

It's not that I'm a dead writer.
I just tend to write
the passed away parts of him back to life.

I'm the scribe before the speaking,
So I suppose I'm his pre-scription.

Bad pun

I apologise.
I'm nervous.
He doesn't let me out on stage much.
Rightly so.
But not from shame though,
he's blameless.
But still responsible.
It's a possible byproduct of social conditioning.
Shirking away the softer underbelly to protect it.
I guess that's why he made me.
Or maybe I made him?
Maybe I'm just a mess-enger.

Don't shoot me for my delivery.

Languishing in this opportunity to live a little more vividly.
Be a little more like him.
You just can't help like him!
The charisma! The smile! The stage presence!
Isn't he just so disarmingly charming!!
So so so talented!
Such a good writer!!
No! I'm the good writer!!
Not just the ghostwriter!!

You know, most writers won't let you see
this part?

Sure you get to see the art.
But never peer into mind of the artist.
See that inner seething **darkness.**
I'm not that dark.

The tortured artist motif is dated.
And frankly, quite problematic.

It gets under my skin
how I live just under his skin.
Have you ever wondered,
what it would be like to be able to perfectly describe the radiance of the sun,
while never having felt it on your own skin?
To live cold in isolation,
then be plated on a stage/gurney.
I as the unknown—a John Doe:
half poet/half cadaver.
The walking dead.
Understudying

the Un-deceased in search of peace,
as most people do.
There
are
a lot of
dead people in the poems I write for him.
So I rewrote this as
a hymn of praise,
that appraises 'I', which is to say 'he/him',
formerly known as 'they'
before the collective became too isolating.
The Id—Myself, and Superego—Me,
Diverging, Polar-I-zed.
Despite deplorable deprecating wordplay,
desperately waiting for the light of day.
Which is to say Son-Rise,
and be the man the father figure said you would be.
*A precursor of *Could be,*
which dispelled the notion of predestination and
allowed for the choice not to.
If,
you so choose.

Day by day, the Monday blues roll on,
And rock to the rhythm of an off-tune beat.
A little out of sync,
so you swim.
Become one with the water you always were,
washing sins away,
waving friends goodbye.

But I
am just his ghostwriter.
So he won't finish this poem.
And you'll never read it.

Ventriloquy Soliloquy

Most of my ideas are better
on paper
I slipped a hand inside myself but
did not feel more in control.

I've been penning pending letters
due for untimely reception.
It is ultimately ineffective.

I read that 'feckless'
is a synonym for 'irresponsible',
but sounds better.

I've used them both here for emphasis.
The point is
moot.
But again, I wrote them anyway,
for the sake of objectivity.
I found that if I called your mouth a cave,
it might make sense for my name
to take shelter in it.

It did not.

Some ideas are better kissed away.
Some words have double meanings.
Some people are not who we intended
they become.

I have come this far, further will not
leave me worse for wear.

Beware
the wor(l)ds.

They spell it out in the most enchanting fashion
and then
mean nothing on purpose.

It is too cruel to say
I told you so.

Yet far too kind
to put it in a poem.

Choose Your Own Adventure
(On trying to write like Shastra Deo)

You wake up on paper

Everything is eggshell white!
Or bone
or some form of collagen calcium composite.

You crane your neck to see the different types of face around you

For once, they're all black!
They're Typefaces
(or is that the same thing as Fonts?)
You never really understood the difference.
It doesn't matter.
You're in a choose your own adventure story!
A choose your own adventure Poem!

Choice:
You continue to the next line. With no sword, just a pen!
Impractical but mightier?

Or
You procrastinate because obviously, you work better under
pressure, and all adjacent menial tasks can be relabelled as research.

You Choose to continue.

You Die

Wake up on paper,

the same eggshell white,

the same black font.

This time you procrastinate.

The poem fast forwards,

carries on developing a life of it's own:

a complex narrative, truth tragedy and trauma,

joy, jubilance, and the potential of a happily ever after.

Choice:

You write something   honest.

Or

You tell a white Lie for validation and to sate your perpetual state
of Un-belonging.

Try poorly to accurately predict what it is that people want or
need to hear.

What you need art to explore! The expressions art is made for!

You tell the truth.

You don't die

but but it feels like it.

You're on a different page now,

same eggshell white same black typeface.

New chapter.

New stanza highlighting the illusion of choice.

You're choosing to push forward.

But you wonder if you ever chose to be here to begin with!

Wasn't that the Original Sin? That whole Eden/apple shenanigan.

The choice that no one ever really had a choice in.

Or is that argument reductive?

Painted in Typeface Black and Eggshell White,

Choice:

You don't choose, you leave it chance, chaos and karma in cyclical
   Samsara

Or

You Advance as both choice maker and the unreliable narrator.
Is this Me or You talking?
Am I the writer? Or the speaker, or the performer?
Or a mirror? Who's choosing the adventure?
Is this a red herring? or a carefully crafted plot twist?

Uh
You missed it, took too long to choose!

You Die!

it's back to paper,
back to the eggshell white, back to black typeface
Trying to make your life into an adventure
and that adventure into a poem.
But you can't seem to make the right

Choice:

You write the perfect ending line, a little triumph, a little loss.
Some sort of moral,
some profound revelatory statement as commentary on
   contemporary society.
A whole lot of growth and a little touch of hope.

Or

You Don't.

Dead Ringer

I'm annoyed by mountains—
the way they mimic molehills. Maybe
it's the other way round?
I tend to bark up the wrong spilt milk.
You can't judge a storm by the size of its teacup.
The details get twisted like the devil in a grain of salt.
Mostly, I bite off more than breaks the ice.
And make hay when it pours.
A chip off the old cold shoulder.
Ignorance comes to those who wait
and adds 1000 words to injury.
The way you can't make an omelette with
all your eggs in the same basket.
And not all that glitters has a silver lining.
Once, two Birds of a feather called the kettle shy,
twice, for the bite.
Both died and blamed a stone. I think?
Your guess is as good as your own medicine,
It tastes like stolen thunder.
And it's hard to make a long story laugh last.
Someone said,
'we were the calm before contempt',
large in our smallness.
It all seems unfamiliar now.
Perhaps we should just let sleeping dogs
change their spots

Breath

Why do lungs make such bad life rafts?
Perhaps,
too porous?
Or too long caged in that bone-meat cavern.
I do not understand how to engage my diaphragm.
Can you imagine living
on involuntary actions?
If survival is a base instinct,
is this a silent death rattle?
All empty air and anguish.
The last time I was winded was age 11.
I have not caught my breath
Since.

Sixth Sense

The first movie I saw with a major plot twist was
The Sixth Sense—
Where we find out Bruce Willis' character was dead the whole time.

That specific twist is a trick I learned to live my life by.
See, addiction is a haunting:
a relentless search for peace by someone who's long been deceased.
A stillborn self-image clawing for a breath of life.
It's making bedmates of death's darkness.
So, step into my shadow.

Where a needle prick, pill drop or whiskey shot acted as a rusty crowbar
trying to pry open my soul.
To feel something.
To feel anything at all.
Anything but dead.
Days turned to nights turned weeks turned to years,
searching to feel alive!
So, of course, I took to poetry,
to hitting line
after line
after line
after lying to myself
after battling denial.
after trying to put together the scattered jigsaw fractal pieces of my mind.

I'm trying to be honest these days,
trying to tell my story like is,
unfiltered, triple distilled just how I like it.

I mean *liked!*
I'm ashamed of how much I liked it.
Of finding an ecstatic sweet relief,
and how that mattered more than living,
mattered more than loving, and all it leaves is longing:
one more hit,
one more sip,
just one kiss,
just tonight,
just forever.
They say we spirits, we live forever.
What that means is that the dying is never-ending
and that the living is spent pretending.
Covering up the pooling crimson quagmire of my fatal wound,
blending in as one of them who assumes,
HIM??
There's no way he could be consumed by phantom antics.
And if he is
call it possession,
a phase,
an escape,
anything to lessen this waking funeral truth.
I buy into it too,
walking both sides of this realm.
An abject detective solving my own murder.
I am both Sisyphus and the boulder.
At the precipice of perception both
the eye and the beholder.
It's impossible to hold the incorporeal closer.
I spend my days hugging wraiths

I faced my inner demons to be haunted by the ghosts of overdoses,
I still hear them screaming,
Thabani call me,
Thabani hold me,
Thabani save me.
I can not save you,
I'm dead too.

But I don't know it.

Getting clean has been a graveyard.
I'm groundskeeper frantically digging,
measuring 6 feet while shovelling twelve steps.
I keep digging,
and digging,
and digging.
My past won't stay buried, but my friends do.
We spectres don't remember who we were before we died.

I'm trying to recover that.

There is no call to action,
no solemn catharsis,
no sympathy for the strung out.
I'm just a kid with a blanket pulled to his chest, talking to ghosts.
And I wonder
if anyone looks at folks like me
croaking the twisted ghastly gasp to ghouls that goes,

I see dead people.

Group Therapy

(He) towers at the door.
More idea than human.
Stoneface,
fractured
by a welcoming smile.

Leads us in.

(We), corralled black sheep,
flock—

the lost in search of healing
in this counterculture cult.

(We) speak clockwise,
taking turns to unburden.

Recount trauma at ten o'clock,

violence at noon,

despair, three through six.

Picked bones, and scratched sores that sought a fix.
In garbled gravel tone,

(He) says we are not broken.

It is hard to hear.

The solemn circle transmutes into a portal.

(We) fall upwards,
backwards
forwards,
into ourselves.

Still seated.
Eyes as headwaters,
feelings as rivers.

(We) came for this flow.

Drinking Buddies

Halfway to nowhere,
holding on to an 'almost there'.
The holy hopeless masquerading as
put together.
Reluctantly an organ donor
with a waitlisted bleeding heart.

'No one needs those anymore'
they said.
I said
'Instead,

make something we can laugh about when it's over.'
But most balms were snake oil,
and most jokes were true.

Most drinks stung too stiff,
We cut wounds with vermouth,
squeezed lime in the lies.
Salt-crusted rims in envy of diamonds,
or the stars we never were.

I swallowed a night sky in hunger for daybreak.
You trapped sunrise in a bottle.

A toast,
to an eternity of tomorrows.

Shibari

Rope is multipurpose.
This makes for varied,
handy,
metaphors.
Adaptable objects are quite
un-specialised.

Mouldable,
malleable,
mutable.

Watch the contortion of knots as
fluidity in things appearing
straight.

Strength is found in weaving parts together.
No sooner a noose than climbing apparatus.

The freest hands I ever touched
were tied.

Overtime

No one came to work today.
Well, I did.
But on paper, I'm more non-person:
trailing without a blaze;
a star,
collapsed into its own gravity,

missing the atmospheric conditions to burn on.
Unremembered in a cubicle universe.

I look up.

The sky glows in fluorescent constellation lines.
Its shine would make cadavers of us all.
For now, no bodies haunt these empty halls.
Keyboard click and clack
tap dances through the silence.

Chain smoking through the lunch break.
I'll breathe clean air when off the clock.
Dying feels better when you're paid for it.
And I'm here for the overtime.

Reflections on Blackness

Can you name this blackness?
This muted onyx hue.
What else lives here with me?
In the empty after hours,
In the unlit silence.

On the border of dreaming and waking,
watch muffled glowing, edging
through cracks and corners.
Low-tone warnings of morning.

They break infinity,
split the continuity of darkness.

Night lights for the children.
Daylight for the working.
Limelight for this starless sky.
A farewell *en noir*.

Naming My Loneliness

I knew the word for this.
      Once.
Back when speaking meant something.
When whispers were more than
me, softly humming to myself.
I spoke with silence today.
She was reticent as ever.
Played this clever trick
to get me talking to the walls.

Silly silence.

The walls are for writing!
Or was it reading?
Or both?

I was leaving or meaning to.

How did I get here?
Wait, no,
I was waiting.

You promised you'd come back.
I promised I would stay.
We said no, to the he-said-she-said games.

I forget,

these days, I'm the only one playing.
Still praying to dead gods and ghost idols.
Too unhinged to hope for miracles.
Too lucid to numb despair.
Calling out to the quietness,
surprised it's only me here.

I fear,
I may never find my way back.
And don't know where to go next.
Is there a word for this?

Midnight Cafe

Empty chairs.
An open door.
Wind chill.
Winter bites.
I wished for this cold all summer.
In the same way,
I wished her away.
Stuck waiting.
Hoping.
Still wishing for difference.

Asymmetric ingratitude,
takes more than you have to give.
Unswept floors.
Print smudged mirrors.
Slow order service.
Why stay home,
when I can live here.

Not a Poet

DON'T CALL ME A POET!!!!!!!
Unless you mean it.
They always say they love you
    but don't mean it.
It's not really a crime,
it's more misdemeanor than felony,
all epitaph and elegy,
with the hymnal assonance of a song sung
to a stained-glass cathedral backdrop.
A crowd of grave faces watch you deliver your own eulogy.
They say they always *loved* your voice.
But don't talk much about the words.
I wonder why?
I wonder will I die
in these dulcet timbre tones
as these lips drip honey gold.
As the poet becomes historian, activist, therapist, part-time
    performing artist, archivist,
and just so fucking sick of it.

Logic says give up,
So naturally, you submit
for publication.
Water down for placating,
amp it up for controversy.
Mix it up to sound the same, but a little different.
You're chasing after fame in all of its glorious iridescence.
If you blink, you just might miss it.
                        I blink.

The auditorium is empty.
I'm not me anymore. I'm just a poet, right?
I'm just this poem right?
Just a piece in pieces right?!
I just wanted to say it right! Right?
So

why
aren't they clapping?

Virtual Disparity

It's highly probable that **none of this is real.**
Everything I think & feel is predetermined.
I'm plugged in.
Impatiently placating, within a state of play.
Life is a game,

This thought does not console me.

My console constantly overheats, from overplay.
My escape is waiting in this station of stasis.

Won't you
stay online a little longer?
Don't leave me so lonely.

Let's co-op one more campaign,
Let's grow up and put the games away
while the external world plays us
as the architects of its own destruction.
Post-apocalyptic survival at its finest.
Filled with enough moral ambiguity to
Appear human.

It's all 1's, zeros & POC NPC's.
The generation that put the 'hyper'-in-realism.
The snow crunch under boots.
The skin slick with sweat.
The blood splatter in a disconcertingly accurate pattern,

None of it is real!

Or at least
that's how history treats violence.
Blame the skin for the damage and ignore
the ultraviolet.
Eyelids flicker, adjusting to the higher resolution.
You never miss a moment,
with the faster shifting frame rate.
My avatar is my namesake.

It is pretending to be me.
I am pretending to be it.
Our performance is pejorative.
We both do what we can
to feel a sense
of free will.

If you will willingly push my buttons,
watch my flawless response time.

Seemingly seamless.
Effectively effortless.

I always find it easier to do what I am told.
I was told it would get easier
the further in I got,
the more I levelled up. The bosses I defeated,
the quests that were completed.

When will the simulation end?

I've spent days overwriting data,
hoping that it would save me.
Living in a screen is the only thing that

saved me.

To respawn in the morning,
until the game is over.

Is
The game over?
Has it only just begun.
Are you ready,

Player 1.

Press X to continue.

Melancholia *En Noir*

'They keep saying, "go slow"'
Do you feel that?
Figure skating on molasses.
Rapid movement fails to prevent the sinking,
your shoes filling, thick and sticky.
You once had to fill these now-filling shoes too.
An unfulfilled endeavour.
You knew better, now know better,
The reintroduction was no better.
The go-getter, who got what they sought.
Yet again, ought to have known better.
And for repetition's sake was still no better,
than when it started.
The real question was why?

First response was 'because'.
In conjunction to being, where the reason,
like the fall, lasted only for a season.
In spite of predestination,
the action was the meaning.
'Too much' was the feeling.

So backtrack.

To a sound so muted, you can't help but hear it.
To piety so disloyal, you counterbalance and revere it.
Iridescent in spectrum, we asked for a larger palette.
Instead were taught absence in black and essence in white.
Contoured with contrite shades of grey.

Enraged,
each prisoner showcased their clanging shackles in protest.
Professing the service of justice be made.
The unsolicited betrothed, and frankly betrayed,
paved the way for a freedom we still fight for today.

So fast-forward.

To crimson rose holes and blue violence.
To white powdered artificial sweetener.
To death.
To departed.
To unplayed vinyls.
To endings, beginnings and things in-between.
Forsaken, foregone, mistaken for unseen.
Resurrected for a select medium.
Imperfect iambic pentameter.
An unwritten sonnet.

Moribund

This is not a thing of beauty.
Nor the abject object of discontent.
It is a clawing, crawling, crippling death.
The reaper and the knell conjoined.
I am not the speaker,
You are not the reader,
We are not who we should be,
anymore.

December 07 1992:

My dearest No-one,

It is your birthday.
This is not a lie.
Nor the truth in its entirety.
You will die soon.
I cannot apologise for inevitability.
All you have yet to achieve is wholly pointless.
The trajectory is set, the compass biased by its own
magnitude.
This life will make marauders of us all.
Do not go home, stay a while.
Leave the kettle to cool, mismatch the socks,
make the most intentional mistakes.
You are worthy of them all.

If you should be so foolish as to fall in love,
write.

Always,
Anyone.

Forget
everything this was meant to be.
Strip the scripting from the scripture.
These hallowed pages were always soaked
in pagan ink,
in forest raven pasted against mute swan.
Congregations likened to flocks,
their hearts tipping against the plume of Ma'at.
Is this all that will remain after
life?

ACT II

INT. CASKET - DAY

THE BODY LIES DORMANT IN THE BLACKNESS, THERE
IS ONLY SILENCE, DECOMPOSING MATTER AND THE
VOID.

NO-ONE:
I expected something more.

CUT TO:

EXT. CEMETERY - NIGHT

THE FUNERAL PROCESSION IS GONE. A LONE
FIGURE LOOMS ABOVE THE FRESH GRAVE. LIGHTS A
CIGARETTE.

NARRATOR (V.O):
Ashes to Ashes, Dust to Despair.

SCENE.

Remember when this sawed us in half?
Did you forget our incorrect expectation?
Our toil to make art from our un-discarded viscera?
Our incompetent exercise in bloodletting?
Left for more modern therapies.
All we wanted was to be known as Men of Letters.
Instead, scrawled illegible scribblings as sigils,
scratched to our eyelids.
Words to ward Charon from our final journey.

Epitaph:
Engraving and entombing are two very different methods
of the same preservation.
May this last an eternity.

Forgive me.
I am as troubled as I am persistent.
As haunted as I am ghostly, or ghastly.
I do not intend to leave destruction in my wake.
These now trampled chrysanthemums
remind me only dead things belong here.
I remain as unseen as a twist of The Ring of Gyges,
unjust in my disappearing.
And for all the time spent mourning, what remains
is this,
not a thing a beauty?

No Strings

I was like you once,
or at the very least,
wished to be with a wistful wile away.
Violently contorted against my will,
a miscarried marionnette.
Birth was labour and, for full circle's sake,
life spent working,
dancing to the strings of a patriarchal puppeteer.
For you,

the gawking voyeur void of intervention.
I, the placid performer,
formed not owning this frame,
responding to clandestine gestures,
just wanting to be a real boy.
But real boys don't cry!

My pseudo-maestro Geppeto
painted a permanent pair of tears on my cheek,
to juxtapose these ivory whites,
archetype-cast in both comedy and tragedy.
These limbs, hand crafted from mahogany and ebony,
know holly is the whitest wood.
And would
replace themselves with lighter-hued lumber for the lick of the
    limelight caress.

Glazed in a chalky veneer,
all dolled up to move to this voodoo.
Uncouth to my culture: taboo to Ubuntu.
Broken Bantu bones thrown
by a wayward witch doctor.
In the way I would doctor my story:
framed to entertain then in seconds be swiftly forgotten.
To drip, drop and drown in the disney+ stream.
My relentless pursuit of personification
reduced to a null hypothesis.
The vagrant voice of a guiding conscience
reverbing as crickets in silence.

While Seeking speech on pleasure island,
I learnt to speak in misdirection where,
half-truths roll off the tongue
with a tastier tang than full lies.
Imitating to flatter, to appease, to assimilate
a little to the party.
While hardly knowing the dance.
But I learned to mirror performing cadence.

Entertain like a human,
can move like a human,
consume like a human,
praise God like a human.
Dear God, I'm not human, but can I be?
Or at least, let me know why you made me?

Who holds to account the callous creator
who selfishly made me a plaything?
The offspring of artists are often abandoned
with a curtain call too late for answers,
and a show that must go on.

'You see,
I had strings but now I'm free
there are no strings on me.'

Seeking Space

Is there space for this?
To laud the orbital
as electrons spin negatively?
Repeating history, each Eve shrouded in the mushroom clouding
    of a split atom to make Eden.

Paved a way with asphyxiation asphalt measured by short breadth.
Buried in false depth.
Its presence, relative to distorted perspective.
Which is to say untimely.

Is the space given or forcefully taken?
Born from the need be,
shed for the need to bleed.
Existing in high demand.

WE supplant ourselves in creative expansion.
Creating space
in half-full rooms for all who care to hear.

Take This.

It is not a gift.
It is sleight of hand, a switch of value.
A trade instead, to sate appropriation.
Take this and leave me be.
Make of it what you will.
Recite it, reply it, rewrite it, clip and crop it,
Photograph it

Screenshot then shoot it off elsewhere.
It was never really here to begin with.
In the same way sin starts with good intentions.

Use it to mean well.
Use it to feel larger, to eclipse, cast shadows,
cast spells, and dispel points of contradiction.
Transmute truths into fiction, sing lies as lullabies.
Take this to bed.
Sleep with it, in it and for it.
Implore it to be more than your imagination
could label it.
Label it.
Highlight for emphasis, annotate for clarity.
Fabricate the varying aspects as a reconstructed reality.
Do it poorly, then badly, then repetitively to perfection.
Dissect approximately one half of the cross-section.
Reflecting on the predilection of wholes taken in part.
Take this apart.
Make it your own.
And I will be mine.

Landlocked

I too am made of waves,
see with saltwater eyes,
am filled with undiscovered depths.
All priceless moments are for sale.
One would wince at the rate.
We steal spent souls on sea shores,
twist tongues around the point of mistruth,
lie on land and with our eyes closed,
feel a gentle rocking.
Are told we are not islands,
but discontent continents.
As a second language speaker of the wind's murmur,
I struggle to make out the wispy mutter.
And wonder what mysteries are lost in translation.
Or reserved to be exchanged with the seaspray—
the secrets in salt and water.

New Year's Day

Prometheus,
do we light the sky with fireworks for you?
Or long to burn the stars?
Or wish to be the stars?
Still starting a new year startled by our own luminescence—
begging to be brighter.

I once saw forever through a phone screen.
A handheld portal
holding the moments I thought I lived through
and instead impartially flicked through.
Neither what my eyes perceived,
nor what the screen revealed,
was more real than the other.
Both mattered and were immaterial.

Since then,
I will remember,
sky lanterns combusting mid-air,
a crowd of no one,
flashing mobile constellations,
my arm around my mother.
Empyrean explosions,
Prometheus forgotten in fireworks.

Give Me (a prayer)

Give me a way to say the unsaid,
to hear the unheard, unburdened by what others may think.
Give me a stiff drink,
or just the throat burn and fire in the belly.
Warm me on cold nights,
love me when it's difficult.
Give me ease.
Not peace, but simplicity in surviving the hardships.
Give me hardship.
Coat my bones in melted ore then toss me in the ocean.
And before I learn to swim,
teach me to drown,
to fight the flooding waters for my life.
Then give me air.
Give me breath.
A sigh of relief, as I am the thief who stole back their life.
Give me life,
as a sentence,
that I may write this story into history.
And when it's old and over-told,
give me nostalgia,
as a propping beam in a falling house,
for me to tell this story one more time.
Give me time,
and I will give you the secrets of this universe.
And at it's end,
give me midnight,
a starless sky,
dark enough to remind me how bright the city lights look when

no one is awake.
I've been awake.
Or more accurately, sleepless.
Or maybe in waking state, not conscious,
but still dreaming

I used to dream,
believing dreams meant more than living.

Fate plays thief of hope
while it holds itself to law.
Time, a devouring flame.
Life, a withering wick.
And I, up in smoke.
With dreams of sunrise.
So give me one more sunrise,
tomorrow.

Tempo

You were the one-
two-three-four, like
tempo count-in, like moved like music, like
count me in,
I was never picked to play. Like
who was good at adolescence anyway? Like
bad jokes, write it off to timing. Like
time stopped or for a second,
I stopped counting.
It was fine. It was five-
six-seven-eight. Like
good choreography and bad dancers. Like
our bodies weren't built to burn this way. Like
how a furnace is just a fireplace with gas. Like
body heat in winter, last winter was so fucking cold.
Last winter, fuck, you called!
It went to voicemail like,
I can't come
to the phone, it's not on vibrate, it's on silent like,
are you listening?
Like leave a message, like leave a like
and subscribe like I said,
it was fine, like
it's fine! Like
everybody's favourite lie, like
you were my favourite line
break.
Wait. That's not quite right like
how you hate that I turn people into poems, like

I can't love them unless they're on the page, like
you're never on the page,
I like it that way,
It keeps you mine.
Nine–ten, like running out of time.
Like opening your eyes.
Like you seek,
and I know where to hide.

Tragicomic (After Sonia)

Ok. You know this one.
A man walks into a bar.
No.
A boy walks into a life.
Into a line.
No.
Two people not quite connected but aligned
No.
A boy walks into a Story.
By now,
he should be better at building.
Still doesn't know the difference
between concrete and cement.
Finds it all to be a little hard.
He never had a home.
Ask him how he put up all those walls.
He always thought plaster
was for broken bones.
He wrote a poem,
to put a cast on a broken heart,
to heal the kind of fracture that feels like drowning.
They called the thing they built a ship
spelt like waterlogged and sinking
out the port with a tattered jib and splintered mast—
just trying to stay afloat.
I was trying to stay afloat.
But isn't it funny how
a buoy is just a boy without
you.

It was just a Boy and You,
and a bunch of bad jokes,
Like

Knock knock?
Who's there?
It's just me.
Me who?
No,
meow like the cat got my tongue again.
Silence
                was the first fist he ever learnt to throw.
So they fought in black and white with slapstick.
All Chaplin, Punch and Judy.
Judge jury and no music. He never played,
But if he did I'd be an Axe-man
Killing softly. With perfect timing.
Crowds love to laugh at Violence
Every night was an open mic,
And 'I love you'
As the perfect stand-up promise for you to fall for.
So romantic!
How their eyes glimmer and gleam by gaslight.
Mourning last night before today's sun goes down
All they ever had was now,
back then,
back when a boy in a bar had a story and a laugh.
They don't laugh much,
anymore.
Not since that last joke.
You know, the one that goes:

Goodbye.

Your Story

So I have this box.
I try to take it most places and, on various occasions,
will work it into any conversation.
It's filled with stories.

Nothing marvellous to look at, about *yay* high,
regular story box size, scuffed on most sides by the mileage of
    mishandling.
You could hold it in the palm of your hand or pop it in your breast
    pocket,
enclose it in a locket laying by your heart with that picture of
someone you'll always love.
Remember *their* story?

How they smile sunshine,
speak in symphony, and smell like those seconds before rainfall?
The memory of them is in the box.

It doesn't lock or have a lid.
No barriers to stop the countless stories pouring in.
But the weird thing is,
they're not my stories.

I want to put my truth inside the box but my truth is either lost or
    incomplete.

Found in the sting of skinned knees.
In cold feet, hesitant to take large steps,
but that remember how it felt to press against warm legs.
If you hear a version of my story,

write me with an ink-less pen,
on paper made from felled fears,
in books bound with bonds of family and friendship
where one is sometimes stronger,
but neither sticks longer than it needs to.

If you need to,

believe that I was more than the things I did.
Keep me in your own story box,
not as the man, but as the myth.
That is my gift to you.
And in exchange,
I'll draw your story from my story box, too.
Let it spin whispers of inspiration around fires on frigid nights.
Tell of your triumphs and your plights,
recounting all the moments, in the beauty of your life.

I have this box,
It's filled with stories.
Inside it you'll live forever.
And with it we'll change the world.
So tell my story.
Maybe this one is one of yours.

A Dream Forgotten

It started
here

               or there

I think.
     I know, I knew,
I'm forgetting.

Letting the letters slip
through those stitched seams of memory.

Upon waking,
the lighter density of dreams makes them seem like reality—
oil floating atop the water.

There was water!
     No.
An endless, maple syrup sea,
but at the time I didn't question the absurdity.

                  To my left,

there was a man with tree bark for pants,
a sort of augmented cyborg
who had razor blades for hands,
with a finger raised proclaiming,

'Now this is cutting edge technology'

In hindsight,
I question it as a form of subconscious social commentary.
Who else would populate our dreams if not we,
projected as unexpected avatars.

Overhead,

a flock of books traverse the effusive purple sky,
squawking the last lines of half-read novels.
Here,
the wind moves like music, repeating a slightly off-tune melody—
a song I once knew, caught on the tip of my tongue,
a moment before forgetting it.
The wind often shuffles from a hypnotic siren song
to ominous banshee scream depending on the humidity.
It is often,
temperate.
Which may come as a surprise,
(the dream realm itself lies adjacent to Hell.)
Explain the relation between Sleep and Death,
and the bleeding through of nightmares.

         I was walking,
 unsure of my destination,
Lumbering along like an undead sprinter,
with that gnawing sensation that
I too was running late.

All clocks
                    moved
counterclockwise,
in stubborn protest demanding universal punctuality.
Minutes became eternity.
Seconds lasted seasons.
Hours were gratuitously given back to us—
as their name suggests.

I think,
I was looking for my namesake.
Thabani means be happy,

Perhaps I was simply seeking joy:
a concept misplaced in the dominion of flesh and bones.
I suppose it makes sense to be found in dreaming,
and melt away on alarm clock cries.

Dreams often lie,
to tell the truth.
What strange fiction.
I think.
            I know,
I knew,
                    And there it goes

Acknowledgements

I would like to thank the Wheeler Centre, where this collection found its genesis during the 2019 Hotdesk fellowship. My 'Artner in Rhyme', Georgia Kartas, with who I regularly wrote many of the pieces here, and who helped in selecting the title. Thank you to the innumerable poets, writers, and artists who have served as a whetstone to sharpen craft and expression, To Shane Strange and Recent Work Press for caring editorial refinement and believing in the work. And my mother, Sheilla Tshuma, for her unconditional support and love.

'Drought Season' appears in the Wheeler Centre Hotdesk
Fellowship Extract 2019
'Broomstrokes 'appears in *Dichotomi Magazine* Edition 02 2020
'S(kin)' appears in the Melbourne City of Literature Poet Laureates
Project 2020
'Overtime' appears in *BareKnuckle Poet Journal of Letters* 2020
'Tragicomic' and 'Tempo' appear in *CUBBYART Magazine* 2021

About the author

Thabani Tshuma is a Zimbabwean writer and performance poet based in Naarm. His work can be found in publications such as *Dichotomi* magazine, *Next in Colour*, *CUBBY ART*, *Cordite Poetry Review*, and ABC ArtWorks' *SLAMMED*. Thabani is co-curator of Thin Red Lines, and recipient of a 2019 Hotdesk fellowship at the Wheeler Centre. He is a featured author with Djed Press. In 2019. he was Slamalamadingdong's 2019 Grand Slam champion, ranked among the top 50 slam poets worldwide at IWPS 2019, and winner of all major awards at the 2019 Melbourne Spoken Word Prize. Writing is the aperture through which he views the world and experiences self in relation to others.